About Author

Mrs. Susan Thomas has 8 years of experience in UFT. She has developed automation frameworks using UFT for large software testing projects. She is strong in VBScript and VBA.

She has worked on projects in below domains.

1. Investment Banking
2. Healthcare
3. Logistics
4. Mortgage Banking
5. Retail Banking

Her hobbies are travelling to new tourist places, watching football, cricket and learning latest technological stuff.

Preface

This book covers all questions on UFT and VBScript. UFT is the most popular automation testing tool in the market today. VBScript is used a scripting language in UFT.

Major Questions covered in this book are.

1. Basics of UFT
2. Variables, data types, Arrays in VBScript
3. Object Repository in UFT
4. Description Programming in UFT
5. Object Repository Manager in UFT
6. Recovery Scenario Manager in UFT
7. Test Settings in UFT
8. Control statements in VBScript
9. String Handling in UFT
10. Maths functions in UFT
11. Date and time functions in UFT
12. Dictionary objects
13. File handling in UFT
14. Error handling in UFT
15. Procedures and functions
16. Classes
17. Regular expressions in Object Repository
18. WSH in UFT
19. WMI in UFT

1. UFT Basics

1.1 Record and playback

1. What are the modes of recording?

There are 3 types of recording modes.

- Analog Recording
- Low Level Recording
- Normal Recording

1.2 Add – in supported

1. What are the different add-ins' supported in UFT?

There are many add-ins' supported in UFT like web, Java, .Net,silverlight

2. What are the default add-ins' in UFT?

In UFT there are 3 default add-ins' viz. activex, visual basic,web

1.3 Licenses
1. What are the types of licenses in UFT?

There are 2 types of licences.

- Seat License
- Concurrent License

2. Test Settings in UFT

Explain Test Settings in UFT.

Test settings is very important part of the UFT test. You can open the test settings from the file sub menu.
You will find below sections in test settings window.

1. Properties Settings:

In properties section you will find the location of the test and add-ins associated with the test.

2. Run Settings:

In run section you will find below settings.

Data table iterations

When error occurs - what to do

Object Synchronization timeout

3. Resources Settings:

In resources section you will be able to see/edit the associated function libraries of the test.

4. Parameters Settings:

In parameters section you will specify the input and ouptu parameters.

You can access the parameters using script as mentioned below.

```
Set qtApp =
CreateObject("QuickTest.Application") '
Create the Application object
Set pDefColl=
qtApp.Test.ParameterDefinitions
Set rtParams = pDefColl.GetParameters()
' Retrieve the Parameters collection
defined for the test.
```

```
Set rtParam = rtParams.Item("sagar") '
Retrieve a specific parameter.
print rtParam.value
```

5. Environment Settings:

In Environment section you can view built - in and user defined global variables. You can also create new user defined variables here.

6. Web Settings:

In web section you can specify the browser navigation timeout.

7. Recovery Settings:

In recovery section you will be able to add and activate/deactivate new recovery scenarios to the test. You can also view the properties of the scenarios.

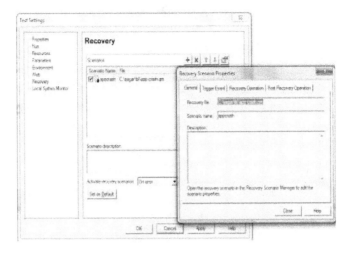

8. Local System Monitor Settings:

In this section you can monitor the various properties of the system like memory usage, cpu usage by given application during test execution.

3. Checkpoints and Output Values

3.1 Checkpoints

Checkpoints are used to verify the property values with expected ones. If they match checkpoints pass else they fail. You can add standard checkpoint by right clicking the statement and then selecting the insert standard checkpoint menu.

Sample checkpoint window is shown in below fig.

```
Browser("Google").Page("Google").WebEdit
("q").Set "salunke"
Browser("Google").Page("Google").WebEdit
("q").Check CheckPoint("q_2")
Browser("Google").Page("Google").WebEdit
("q").Output CheckPoint("q")
Browser("Google").Page("Google").WebButt
on("Google Search").Click
```

3.2 Output Values

Output value is used to store the data generated by application while execution is going on for later use. For example - Suppose after you place the order, order id is generated. So you can store this order id in output value so that you can use this value for later use to fax the order. To add the output value you have right click on the statement after which you want to add output value. Once you right click you will find the output value properties window like the one below.

14

You can check the property values that you want to store in the output value. You can also specify where you want to store the values (Data table or environment)

```
Browser("Google").Page("Google").WebEdit
("q").Set "salunke"
Browser("Google").Page("Google").WebEdit
("q").Output CheckPoint("q")
Browser("Google").Page("Google").WebButt
on("Google Search").Click
```

4. Object Repository

4.1 Local OR

1. What is the Difference between local and shared object repository (OR) in UFT?

Object repository is used to store the test object and its properties/values. There are 2 types of Object Repositories.

- Local
- Shared

Difference between local and shared OR is given below

- Local OR is used by only one action in Test While Shared OR can be used by multiple actions and tests
- Local OR can be edited without OR manager While shared OR can be edited by using only OR manager
- We cannot merge 2 local OR but we can merge 2 shared ORs using OR manager
- We cannot compare 2 local OR but we can compare 2 shared ORs using OR manager
- We can associate/disassociate the shared OR to test at run time but Local OR is associated to test at any time by default.
- Extension of the shared OR is .tsr while Local OR is .mtr
- When we export the Local OR, shared OR is created.

4.2 Shared OR

1. What is the use of object repository manager in UFT?

Object repository manager in UFT is very important tool to manage the shared object repository. Please note that you can't use Object repository manager in UFT to manage local object repository.

Below are the main uses of Object repository manager in UFT.

- Open and edit shared object repository (TSR files).
- Compare 2 shared Object repositories in UFT.
- Merge 2 shared Object repositories in UFT.

2. How to Associate Object Repository to UFT Test?

Well - we can associate object repository to UFT Test either manually or by automation code.

Manually with Test Settings - In this method you have to go to Resources->Associate repositories. Here you can give the path of tsr file that is Shared OR.

By Automation Code, You have to use repositories collection object as mentioned in below code.

```
Dim UFTAPP

Dim qtObjRes

Set UFTAPP=
CreateObject("QuickTest.Application")

UFTAPP.Launch
UFTAPP.Visible = True
```

```
UFTAPP.Open "C:\Test\Testabc", False,
False

Set qtObjRes = UFTAPP.Test.Actions
("Login").ObjectRepositories

qtObjRes.Add "C:\OR\myRes.tsr", 1
```

3. How to create a Shared Object Repository in UFT?

Please follow the steps given below to create a shared Object Repository in UFT.

Open Local Or

Go to File->Export Local Objects

Save file as abc.tsr

So abc.tsr will be a shared OR and we can associate it with any test.

5. Descriptive Programming

5.1 Static

1. When to use descriptive Programming in UFT?

Descriptive programming in UFT is used in below scenarios.

Whenever the objects in the applications change quite often.

When it is not feasible to store the objects in OR. For example all links on the page

When same object exists in the different pages/windows of the application.

There are 2 types of description programming.

Static Descriptive programming

Dynamic Descriptive programming

Static Descriptive programming Example –

```
Browser("index:=0").page("title:=Google"
).webedit("name:=q").set "xyz"
```

Dynamic Descriptive programming Example –
```
'Find all edit boxes on google page using
descriptive programming
```
```
Set descriptionObject =
Description.Create()
```

```
descriptionObject("micclass").value =
"webedit"
descriptionObject("outerhtml").value =
".*input.*"
descriptionObject("outerhtml").regularex
pression = true

set col =
Browser("index:=0").page("title:=Google"
).childobjects(descriptionObject)
print "Total edit boxes on the page" &
col.count
For i=0 to col.count-1
  print col(i).getROProperty("outerhtml")
Next
```

5.2 Dynamic

1. **How to use regular expression in descriptive programming in UFT?**

As we know that there are 2 ways of descriptive programming.

1. Static
2. Dynamic

We can use regular expression in both the ways as mentioned below. Please note that by default all the property values are considered as regular expressions by UFT.

Regular Expressions in Static descriptive programming in UFT.

```
Browser("index:=0").page("title:=Google"
).Webedit("name:=q").set "sagar salunke"
```

```
Browser("creationtime:=0").page("title:=
Google").Webbutton("name:=Google.*").Cli
ck
```

Please note that last statement uses regular expression to identify the button whose name starts with Google.

If your property value itself contains the special character then that should be escaped using \ character.

Example - Suppose you want to click on the link "+sagar".
Now this link contains the special character +. To click on this link, we can use below code

```
Browser("creationtime:=0").page("title:=
Google").Link("innertext:=\+sagar").Clic
k
```

Regular Expressions in Dynamic descriptive programming in UFT.

```
Set descriptionObject =
Description.Create()
descriptionObject("innertext").value =
"+sagar"
descriptionObject("innertext").RegularEx
pression = false
```

Please note that we can specify whether the value is regular expression or not using RegularExpression property. By default it is true.

```
Browser("index:=0").page("title:=Google"
).Link(descriptionObject ).click
```

This is how we can use Regular Expressions in UFT

6. Recovery Scenario Manager

6.1 Recovery Scenario Wizard

1. What are the steps in creating recovery scenario?

Open Recovery Scenario Manager.Using recovery scenario manager you can create new recovery scenarios and store it in a file with .qrs extension. One qrs file may contain multiple recovery scenarios. To create new recovery scenario, click on the button circled with red color. It will open recovery scenario wizard.

Open Recovery Scenario Wizard.Recovery scenario wizard shows the steps involved in creating the recovery scenario. Click on Next

Select Trigger Event.There are 4 types of the trigger events.

1. Pop up window
2. Object State
3. Test Run Error
4. Application Crash

Specify the trigger Details. In this step you have to specify more details about the trigger. For example if you selected pop up window in trigger event above, you will have to provide the title or text of the pop up as shown below.

Recovery Operation. After specifying the trigger event, you have to provide the recovery operation. There are 4 types of the recovery operations.

1. Keyboard or mouse operation
2. Close application process
3. Function Call
4. Restart Microsoft Windows

Post Recovery Operation.

In Post Recovery You can tell what step should be executed after recovery is done by UFT.

Name the Recovery Scenario.

You have to give the name to recovery scenario in this step

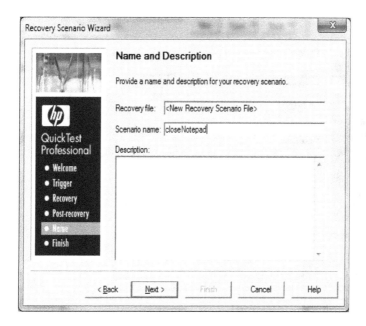

Finishing the recovery scenario.

This is last step. You can add this scenario to current test in this step.

Once you click finish recovery scenario manager window will be shown where you can save the qrs file.

Please note that to activate recovery scenario, you have to go to test settings.

7. Excel and Data tables in UFT

7.1 Excel

1. How to import excel sheet to data table in UFT?

When we design a test automation framework in UFT, we usually store the test data inside excel sheets.
Sometimes we need to load the test data in datatable to execute the test cases.

We can either import all excel sheets from excel workbook or we can import particular excel sheet from the the workbook to the datatable

To import all sheets from excel file, use below line of code

```
datatable.Import "c:\abc.xls"
```

To import single sheet from excel file, use below line of code
Here we are importing the sheet global from **abc.xls** into testdata sheet in Data table in UFT.

```
datatable.AddSheet "testdata"
datatable.ImportSheet
"c:\abc.xls","Global","testdata"
```

2. How to read a value from Excel cell in UFT?

Below script will read data from excel file

```
filepath  = "C:\Bugs\Report.xlsx"
Set objExcel  =
createObject("Excel.Application")
objExcel.Visible = True
Set Wb =
objExcel.Workbooks.Open(filepath)
print Wb.worksheets(1).Cells(1,1).Value
```

7.2 Data tables

1. How to export datatable to excel Sheet?

Add some data to global sheet in datatable

```
datatable.GlobalSheet.AddParameter
"p1","v"
datatable("p1") = "abc"
```

Export complete datatable - This will export all sheets from the datatable

```
datatable.Export("c:\abc.xls")
```

Export only particular sheet from the datatable to excel sheet
After below code is executed, sheet with name global will be
exported to excel sheet in kk.xls

```
datatable.ExportSheet"c:\kk.xls","Global
"
```

8. Databases in UFT

8.1 Microsoft Access

How to get data from the access data base in UFT?

Code below can be used to read data from database in UFT.

```
Set db =
createobject("ADODB.Connection")
db.Open
"Provider=Microsoft.Jet.OLEDB.4.0;Data
Source=G:\priyanka\vb6\admission_project
.mdb;Persist Security Info=False"

Set rst= createobject("ADODB.Recordset")
rst.Open "select * from Course ", db,3

id = rst.RecordCount

For i=0 to id-1

    print rst.fields(0) & rst.fields(1)
& rst.fields(2) & rst.fields(3)
    rst.Movenext

Next
```

How to insert a record or data into database in UFT?

Code below can be used to insert data into database in UFT.

```
Set cn= createobject("ADODB.Connection")
cn.Open
"Provider=Microsoft.Jet.OLEDB.4.0;Data
Source=G:\priyanka\vb6\admission_project
.mdb;Persist Security Info=False"
Set rst =
createobject("ADODB.Recordset")
cn.execute "insert into
table(column1,column2) values
(colvalue1,colvalue2)"
```

9. Utility Objects in UFT

9.1 Reporter

1. Explain Reporter Object in UFT.

Reporter object is used to log the pass/fail status of the step to the results.

We can use below syntax for logging the results.

```
Reporter.ReportEvent EventStatus,
ReportStepName, Details [,ImageFilePath]
```

9.2 DotNetFactory

1. Explain DotNetFactory Object in UFT.

In UFT, you can use dotnetfactory object to access .net objects. You must have .net framework installed in your system before you use createinstance method.

It enables you to create an instance of a .NET object, and access its methods and properties. Createinstance method returns a COM interface for a .NET object.

Syntax

```
Set myobj = DotNetFactory.CreateInstance
(TypeName [,Assembly] [,args])
```

HereTypename - any type name that .net framework provides

Example :

The following example uses the CreateInstance method to create a object of a system environment type

```
Set obj =
Dotnetfactory.CreateInstance("System.Env
ironment")
print obj.MachineName
```

10. File Handling in UFT

10.1 Files

1. How to read a text file in UFT?

How to Read a text file in UFT

Example -

Below code will Read a text file in UFT

```
Set fso =
CreateObject("Scripting.FileSystemObject
")
 Set f =
fso.OpenTextFile("c:\mytestfile.txt", 1)
print  f.ReadAll
```

Above code will read all data from c:\mytestfile.txt file and print it in UFT.

2. How to create a text file in UFT?

Below Code will create a text file in UFT

```
Set fso =
CreateObject("Scripting.FileSystemObject
")
```

```
Set MyFile =
fso.CreateTextFile("d:\mytestfile.txt",
True)
MyFile.WriteLine("This is my  test.")
MyFile.Close
```

This is how we can create a text file in UFT.

How to write contents to text file in UFT

Example -

Below Code will write all data in contents variable to text file in UFT

```
content = "This will be in file "

Set Fo= createobject("Scripting.
FilesystemObject")

Set f=
Fo.openTextFile("c:\abc.txt",8,true)

  f.Write (contents)
  f.Close
 Set f = nothing
```

10.2 Folders

How to create a folder in UFT?

Below code will create a folder in UFT

```
Environment.Value("ResultFolderPath") =
"C:\myf"
Set Fo =
createobject("Scripting.FilesystemObject
")
If Not
Fo.FolderExists(Environment.Value("Resul
tFolderPath")) Then
      Fo.CreateFolder (
Environment.Value("ResultFolderPath") )
End If
```

11. Web applications and HTML DOM in UFT

How to Use HTML DOM in UFT?

Using html DOM you extract all kind of information from web page as you can access source code of the page in the form of HTML.

HTML DOM has many method and properties associated with it like getElementById, nextsibling etc.

To access these methods you must create the DOM object first.

```
Set domObject =
Browser("myb").Page("myp").object
```

Above statement will create the DOM object for the page called myp.

Now let us use the dom object we have created above to get more information of the page currently displayed in the application.

```
Print
domObject.getElementById("myid").innerTe
xt
  ' Prints the text inside the Element -
myid
Print
domObject.getElementById("myid").innerHT
ML
   ' Prints the inner HTML of Element -
myid
```

How to access the parent object of given DOM Object

You can also find the parentobject, nextsibling, previoussibling of the given dom object using built in properties as mentioned below.

```
Set parentObj =
domObject.getElementById("myid").parentN
ode  ' gets the parent object of myid
Set nextsiblingObj =
domObject.getElementById("myid").nextsib
ling 'gets the next sibling object of
myid
Set previoussiblingObj =
domObject.getElementById("myid").previou
ssibling
```

For complete list of methods you can visit http://www.w3schools.com/jsref/dom_obj_node.asp

How to get the collection of all TD (table data cells) elements of the table using HTML DOM in UFT?

```
Set tdtags
=Browser("a").Page("p").WebTable("t").Ob
ject.getElementsByTagName("TD")
```

How to get the collection of all TH (table header cells) elements of the table using HTML DOM in UFT?

```
set thtags =
Browser("abc").Page("mypage").WebTable("
```

```
mytable") .Object.getElementsByTagName("T
H")
```

How to get the value of attribute of any element using HTML DOM in UFT?

```
Set myobj =
Browser("abc").Page("mypage").WebTable("
mytable").Object
Print myobj.getAttribute("class")
'This will print the value of class
attribute of myobj  - table
```

How to get the collection of all table rows using HTML DOM in UFT?

```
Set tableObj
=Browser("abc").Page("mypage").WebTable(
"mytable").Object
Set trtags =
tableObj.getElementsByTagName("tr")
```

How to find the total number of rows in table Using HTML DOM in UFT?

```
print trtags.length
```

How to get the value inside table cell Using HTML DOM in UFT?

```
Set tdtags
=Browser("abc").Page("mypage").WebTable(
"mytable").Object.getElementsByTagName("
TD")
```

```
Print tdtags(0).innerText
'print the text displayed inside first
td tag in table
```

What is previousSibling, nextSibling in UFT?

Well - let me tell you that all the properties (previousSibling, nextSibling) are not defined by UFT.

All these properties are HTML DOM properties that help us get the elements at the same level of the given element in web page.

You can access these method in UFT using .object property which lets you access native methods and properties of the objects/elements.

Example -

```
<body>
<div id="parentdiv">
 This text is inside div element of
which id is - parentdiv

<div id="fc">
 This is nested div1
</div>


<div id="sc">
 This is nested div2.
</div>
```

```
</div>
</body>
```

As you can see in above example, 2 div elements (fc, sc) are inside the div(parentdiv).

So for fc-div and sc-div, parentdiv is the parent element. While for parentdiv, fc-div and sc-div are child div elements. The div elements fc-div and sc-div are siblings of each other as both are at same level.

sc-div is the nextSibling of the fc-div. While fc-div is the previousSibling of the sc-div.

You can get access to these elements using HTML DOM properties nextSibling, previousSibling properties

For example –

```
'access the next sibling of fc-div
set obj=
Browser("myb").Page("myp").object.getEle
mentById("fc")
print obj.nextSibling.innerText

'access the previous Sibling of sc-div
set obj=
Browser("myb").Page("myp").object.getEle
mentById("sc")
print obj.previousSibling.innerText
```

What is parentNode, childNodes, firstChild, lastChild in UFT?

Well - let me tell you that all the properties (parentNode, childNodes, firstChild, lastChild) are not defined by UFT.

46

All these properties are HTML DOM properties that help us get the child and parent element of the given element in web page.

You can access these method in UFT using .object property which lets you access native methods and properties of the objects/elements.

Example –

```
<body>
<div id="parentdiv">
 This text is inside div element of
which id is - parentdiv

<div id="fc">
 This is nested div1
</div>

<div id="sc">
 This is nested div2.
</div>

</div>
</body>
```

As you can see in above example, 2 div elements (fc, sc) are inside the div(parentdiv).
So for fc-div and sc-div, parentdiv is the parent element. While for parentdiv, fc-div and sc-div are child div elements.

You can get access to these elements using HTML DOM properties parentNode, childNodes, firstChild, lastChild.

For example –

```
'access the child objects
set divParentObject=
Browser("myb").Page("myp").object.getEle
mentById("parentdiv")
print
divParentObject.firstChild.innerText
print
divParentObject.lastChild.innerText

set allchilds =
divParentObject.childNodes
for i=0 to allchilds.length-1
 print allchilds(i).innerText
next

'access the parent element of div with
id "fc"
set childObject =
Browser("myb").Page("myp").object.getEle
mentById("fc")

print childObject.parentNode.innerText
```

What is getElementsByTagName in UFT?

If you are testing web application, you may have
used getElementsByTagName method to get access to all
elements that have given tag.

Please note that this is not UFT's own method but it is native
HTML DOM method.

getElementsByTagName takes one parameter as an input which should be the tag of the element like td, tr, span, div etc. This method returns the collection of elements that have the given tagname.

Example.

```
<body>
<div id="head">
 This text is inside div element of
which id is - head
</div>

<div>
 This is another div
</div>

<div>
 This is div number 3.
</div>

</body>
```

In above example, we have sample html document body in which there are 3 div elements.

To get the text value inside all these div elements, we can use the innertext method as mentioned below.

```
set tn =
```

```
Browser("myb").Page("myp").object.getEle
mentsByTagName("DIV")
for i=0 to tn.length-1
    'print the innertext of each div
element here
    print tn(i).innerText
next
```

Thus basically we use getElementsByTagName method to get all element objects with given tag name.

How to use getElementById in UFT?

I know that you have come on this page because you are testing the web application.
Web application testing is very interesting stuff.

Apart from normal web methods and properties provided by UFT, you can use lot of native methods of the web elements.

One of such native method of the document object is getElementById.
This method takes one parameter as an input which should be the id of the element.

Example.

```
<body>
<div id="head">
 This text is inside div element of
which id is - head
</div>
</body>
```

In above example, we have sample html document body in which there is one div element with id = 'head' and it contains some text.

To get the value inside this div element, we can use the innertext method as mentioned below.

```
print
Browser("myb").Page("myp").object.getEle
mentById("head").innerText
```

So output of above code will be.

"This text is inside div element of which id is - head"

Thus basically we use getElementById method to get the element object and then we can use its innerText method to get the data inside that element.

Please note that we can also get the data inside hidden elements using this method. UFT can not read data inside hidden elements.

How to get innerText of webelement in UFT?

In my 10 years of experience in UFT, I have worked on many web applications that involved jquery, ajax and rich controls.

To test such applications we must have good understanding of the HTML DOM concept.
Extracting the values from the web elements on the page is very common thing that we do in UFT.

To get the inner text or inner html of the web elements, we can use below syntax.

Example –

```
print
browser("bb").page("xys").Object.getElem
entById("pqr").innerText
```

Please note that we should use the .object after property before we use html dom.

In above example I am trying to get the text displayed inside web element of which id is "pqr"

We can use more such methods as mentioned below to get access to the web elements on the page
1. getElementById() - get the element by id
2. getElementsByTagName() - get all elements with given tag name
3. getElementsByClassName() - (does not work in < ie9) - get all elements having given class
4. getAttribute() - get the value of attribute of given node
5. getAttributeNode() - get the attribute node
6. hasAttribute() - check if a node has given attribute
7. hasChildNodes() - check of node has any children
8. item() - access the node based on the index from the collection

Once we get the element object, we can use below properties

to get the data.

1. innerHTML – gets the html code inside element
2. innerText - gets the text value inside element
3. getAttribute – gets the value of attribute
4. nodeName - (like TD, SPAN, #text, #document, Attribute name)
5. nodeType - (Element, Text, Attribute, Comment, Document)
6. nodeValue - (attribute Value)
7. childNodes - gets all child elements of the given node
8. attributes - gets the collection of all attributes of given node
9. className - gets the name of class of given element
10. firstChild - gets the access to first child element of the given node.
11. Id – gets the id of the given node.
12. lastChild – gets the last child element of the given node
13. nextSibling – gets the next element at the same level as given node.
14. offsetLeft
15. offsetTop
16. previousSibling - – gets the previous element at the same level as given node.
17. parentNode –gets the parent node of the given node
18. scrollLeft
19. scrollTop
20. scrollWidth
21. style - gets the style information of the given node
22. tagName – gets the name of the tag of given node
23. textContent – gets the text displayed inside given node
24. title - gets the title of the given node
25. length – gets the total number of nodes in the collection.

This is how we can use html dom in UFT to get the information displayed on the webpage. This makes the web application testing quite easy stuff.

12. Framework Designing in UFT

12.1 Types of frameworks

1. What are the types of automation frameworks in UFT?

Types of Automation Frameworks in UFT

Automation framework is designed to ease the process of test automation using UFT. Automation framework helps from scalability point of view. It is very easy to automate the test cases using automation framework rather than ad hoc approach.

There are mainly 3 types of Automation Frameworks in UFT

- Keyword Driven Framework
- Data Driven Framework
- Hybrid Framework

Keyword Driven Framework :
In Keyword Driven Framework , Importance is given to functions than Test Data. when we have to test multiple functionality we can go for keyword frameworks. Each keyword is mapped to function in UFT library and application.

DATA Driven Framework :
In data driven framework, importance is given to test data than multiple functionality of application. We design data driven framework to work with applications where we want to test same flow with different test data.

Hybrid Framework -
This is the combination of keyword and data driven frameworks.

After analyzing the application, you can decide what kind of framework best suits your needs and then you can design automation framework in UFT.

12.2 Components of framework

1. Explain keyword driven automation framework in UFT?

Keyword driven Automation Framework is most popular UFT framework. It is very easy to design and learn a keyword driven automation framework in UFT.

In this article I will explain you all details about how we can design and use keyword driven automation framework in UFT with example. I will also explain the advantages and disadvantages of keyword driven automation framework in UFT. In keyword driven automation framework, focus is mainly on kewords/functions and not the test data. This means we focus on creating the functions that are mapped to the functionality of the application.

For example - Suppose you have a flight reservation application which provides many features like

- Login to the application
- Search Flights
- Book Flight tickets
- Cancel Tickets
- Fax Order
- View Reports

To implement the keyword driven automation framework for this kind of application we will create functions in vbscript for each functionality mentioned above. We pass the test data and test object details to these functions.

The main components of keyword driven automation framework in UFT

Each keyword driven automation framework has some common components as mentioned below.

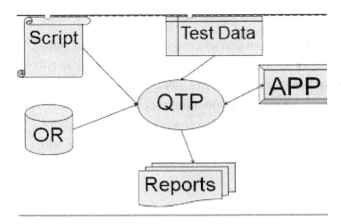

As dispalyed in above image, We have 5 main components in **keyword driven automation framework**

1. Scripts Library (.vbs, .txt, .qfl)
2. OR - Object Repository
3. Test Data (generally in excel format)
4. UFT - Settings and Environment Variables
5. Reports - (Generally in HTML format)
6. Test Driver Script/ Test Engine

Please explain how Test Data sheet looks like in keyword driven automation framework in UFT.

Generally automated test cases are stored in excel sheets. From UFT ,we read excel file and then row by row we execute the functions in a test case. Each test case is implemented as a set of keywords.

Common columns in Data sheet are mentioned below.

- Test case ID - Stores the Test Case ID mapped to Manual Test Cases.
- Test Case Name - Name of the Test cases/ Scenario.
- Execute Flag - if Marked Y -> Test case will be executed
- Test_Step_Id - Steps in a test case
- Keyword - Mapped to function in library file.
- Object Types - Class of the object e.g winedit, webedit, swfbutton etc
- Object Names -Names of objects in OR .
- Object Values - Actual test data to be entered in the objects.
- Parameter1 - This is used to control the execution flow in the function.

Test_ID	TC_Name	Execute	Test_Step_ID	Keyword	Object_Types	Object_Names	Object_Values	Parameter1
1	Login To App	Y	Step1	login	winedit;winedit	userid;password	salunke;mercury	
			Step2	Insert_Order	wincombobox;wincombobo	flyfrom;flyto	london;paris	
			Step3	Fax_Order				Order_Id

Please note that this is just a sample data sheet that can be used in keyword driven framework. There could be customized data sheets for each project depending upon the requirement and design.

For example there could be more parameters or test data is stored in the databases.

Please explain Test Driver Script in UFT.

This is the heart of keyword driven / data driven frameworks. This is the main script that interacts with all modules mentioned above.

Main tasks that are accomplished by driver script are ->

- Read data from the Environment variables /File or from ini file.
- Call report module to create Report folders / files
- Import Excel sheet to Data table.
- Read Excel file.
- Call the function mapped to keyword.
- Log the result

13. Error Handling and debugging in UFT

13.1 Error Handling

How to do Error Handling in UFT?

There are 2 ways in which we can handle errors in UFT.

- Err object.
- Recovery Scenarios.

Sample code to handle the error is given below

```
If err.number <> 0 Then
print err.description
else
print "there  was  no  error  in  above
statement"
end if
```

Whenever any error occurs in the script, We get the message window with detailed description of the error.

But when we are executing the scripts, we do not want this message box to appear to come as this will halt the execution of the script.

To prevent message box from appearing, we use below statement above the block of code.

On error resume next

----

more statements

With On error resume next in place, UFT script runs even though error exists in the code. We can capture those errors using Err object as stated earlier.

When you are debugging the scripts, you should not use On error resume next statement as it will suppress the errors and you will not be able to figure out the issue in your script.Sample code to handle the error is given below

```
If err.number <> 0 Then
print err.description
else
print "there  was  no  error  in  above
statement"
end if
```

Whenever any error occurs in the script, We get the message window with detailed description of the error.

But when we are executing the scripts, we do not want this message box to appear to come as this will halt the execution of the script.

To prevent message box from appearing, we use below statement above the block of code.

On error resume next

----

more statements

With *On error resume next* in place, UFT script runs even though error exists in the code. We can capture those errors using Err object as stated earlier.

When you are debugging the scripts, you should not use On error resume next statement as it will suppress the errors and you will not be able to figure out the issue in your script.

14. UFT and VbScript

When do we use Cdate and Cstr in UFT?

Cdate and Cstr are data type conversion functions in UFT.

For Example -

CDATE

```
DOB = "09-jan-1986"
myDate = CDate(DOB)
myDate will have date data type.

Cstr
a = 10
mystring = cstr (a)
```

mystring will have data type as String....

Explain DateDiff function in UFT.

DateDiff function is used to find out the difference between 2 dates.

For example -

Suppose you know the date of birth of someone and want to find out the age of that person, you can use datediff function in this case.

```
DateDiff (Interval_Type, Date1, Date2)
```

Here Interval Type can be of below types.

yyyy - Year
m - Month
d - Day
h - Hour
n - Minute
s - Second

Example –

```
dateofbirth ="09-01-1986"
print datediff("yyyy", dateofbirth ,now)

'This will print your age in years
```

What are the different String functions in UFT?

Here is the list of all string functions in UFT.

String functions to extract the part of the string -

- **left** - gets the specified number of characters from the left side of string
- **mid** -gets the specified number of characters from the given position of the string
- **right** - gets the specified number of characters from the right side of string

String functions to remove the spaces from the string -

- **ltrim** - removes the blank spaces from the left side of the string
- **rtrim** - removes the blank spaces from the right side of the string
- **trim** - removes the blank spaces from the left and right side of the string

Other String functions -

- **String** - Returns a string of the given length with specified character.
- **Space** - Returns the empty string with given length
- **strReverse** - Reverses the given string
- **ucase** - Converst the string to upper case
- **lcase** - Converts the string to lower case
- **strComp** - Compares 2 strings
- **replace** - replaces the given string str1 from input string say str with other string say str2
- **len** - gets the number of characters in given string
- **split** - splits the string into array using given delimiter
- **join** - forms the string from given array elements
- **cstr** - converts the data type of the variable into String
- **chr** - gets the character corresponding to the given ascii value
- **Asc** - gets the ascii value of the given character.
- **instr** - searches for a substring in a given string and returns the position where the match is found.

- **InStrRev**- searches for a substring in a given string and returns the position where the match is found from the end of the string.

Explain replace function in UFT with Example.

Replace function is used to replace the part of the given string with other sub string in UFT.

Example -

```
myString = "Sachin plays cricket"

print replace(myString,"Sachin","Dhoni")
'Will print Dhoni plays cricket

print replace(myString,"sachin","Dhoni")
'Will print Sachin plays cricket.
Because we have used sachin in small
case letter

print
replace(myString,"sachin","Dhoni",1,-
1,0)
'Will print Sachin plays cricket
.....Same as above

print
replace(myString,"sachin","Dhoni",1,-
1,1)
'Will print Dhoni plays cricket....
```

```
'The last parameter of replace
determines whether the replacement is
case-sensitive or case-insensitive.
'If last parameter is 0, replacement is
case-sensitive
'If last parameter is 1, replacement is
case-insensitive
```

Syntax –

```
replace(myString,"replacethis","replace
with",startat,count,comparisonmehtod)
```

Parameter1 - myString - > String to be scanned and modified
Parameter2 - replacethis- > String to be searched and replaced for
Parameter3 - replacewith- > String to be replaced with
Parameter4 - startat- > from what position the myString should be searched...Default is 1.
Parameter5 - count- > How many replacements should be done. Default is -1 - All occurrences
Parameter6 - comparisonmehtod- > Is comparison case-sensitive?..Default is 0 - binary comparison.

Explain right, mid, left functions in UFT with Examples.

UFT supports lot of string functions.
Some of the commonly used string manipulation functions are given below.

1. right
2. mid

3. left

All of the above functions are frequently used when performing any string operations in UFT.

All of the above functions extract the part of the string / Sub string.

Right function returns the fixed number of characters from right side of the string.

Left function returns the fixed number of characters from left side of the string.

Mid function can be used to get the characters/ sub string from the left, right or middle part of the string.

Examples –

```
myString = "Sachin Plays Cricket"

print right(myString,7)
'will return the 7 characters from the
right side of myString
'Cricket
print left(myString,6)
'will return the 6 characters from the
left side of myString
'Sachin
print mid(myString,8,5)
'will return the 5 characters from the
8th position of myString
'Plays
```

Syntax -

Second parameter in left and right function tells how many characters to return from the string.

In mid functions there are 2 parameters. First parameter tells from which position of the string we have to get the characters and second parameter tells how many characters to return.

Explain Ubound function in UFT.

Ubound stands for upper bound. This functions is used to find the upper bound of the array.

Syntax –

```
ubound(arrayname, dimension)
```

It returns the upper bound of the arrayname and dimension used is specified in second parameter.
By default dimension is 1.

Example -

<u>Single dimension array</u>

```
Dim a(2)
'Declare an array with upper bound
(index) as 2.

a(0) = 0
a(1) = 0
a(2) = 0
```

```
print ubound (a)          'will print 2
print ubound (a,1)        'will print 2

'This will print the value 2 as upper
bound of the array is 2.
```

How to create a array of dictionary in UFT?

In UFT and vbscript we can create array of dictionary using below syntax/ example.

```
dim ArrayofDictionary(2)

'Now let us make first element of array
as dictionary

Set ArrayofDictionary(0)=
createobject("scripting.dictionary")
ArrayofDictionary(0).Add "key1", "temp1"
ArrayofDictionary(0).Add "key2", "temp2"

'Added keys in first dictionary


'Now let us make second element of array
as dictionary

Set ArrayofDictionary(1)=
createobject("scripting.dictionary")
ArrayofDictionary(1).Add "key1", "temp1"
ArrayofDictionary(1).Add "key2", "temp2"
```

'Added keys in second dictionary

and so on ....

To access the values inside dictionary, use below syntax.

```
print ArrayofDictionary(1)("key2")
```

How to remove the spaces from string in UFT

Example -

To remove the spaces from string in UFT, you can use replace function.

```
print replace(" sdsd sd sd s ","
"," ")
```

```
' Output will be sdsdsdsds
```

If you want to remove only leading spaces from string then you can use ltrim function

```
print ltrim(" sdsd sd s ")
```

```
'Output will be "sdsd sd s "
```

If you want to remove only trailing spaces from string then you can use rtrim function

```
print rtrim(" sdsd sd s ")
```

'Output will be " sdsd sd s"

What is early binding and late binding in UFT

In UFT, all variables of variant type. Meaning It is not necessary to declare a variable with any data type like int, float etc.

When we initialize a variable with any value, UFT will assign a data type to that variable depending upon what kind of Value is assigned to the variable.

Example –

```
Dim a
a = 10
```

In above code, when we assign the value of 10 to a, data type of a becomes integer.
This means that at runtime, the data type binding is happening. This is called as a late binding in UFT.

how to find yesterday's date in UFT?

Below code will find out yesterday's date in UFT .

```
print DateAdd("d",-1,date)
```

Please note that you can find any past or future date using above function. The second parameter is used to specify the interval number.

For example - If you specify 1, it will give you tomorrow's date. If you specify -2, it will give you the date one day before yesterday.

15. Miscellaneous Questions in UFT

This chapter will cover some other questions on UFT.

1. How to send an email from Outlook in UFT?

Code mentioned below will send mail to aTO from outlook.

```
Set Outlook =
CreateObject("Outlook.Application")
Dim Message 'As Outlook.MailItem
Set Message =
Outlook.CreateItem(olMailItem)
With Message
.Subject = Subject
.HTMLBody = TextBody
.Recipients.Add (aTo)
Const olOriginator = 0
.Send
End With
```

2. How to use Regular Expressions in OR in UFT?

Object repository stores the test object properties and their values. We can use regular expressions to set the values of the properties of the test object.

When we use the value as a regular expression, single test object in OR can be be used to find the multiple run time objects.

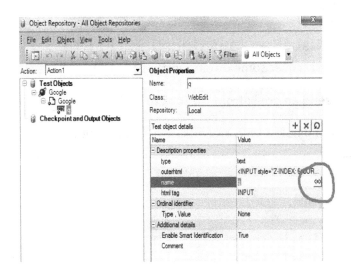

For Example -

As shown in above image, we need to click on the button (circled with red) in front of the property value that you want to make as a regular expression. After you click that button, you will get below window

Then we need to enter the regular expression in the edit box and check the regular expression checkbox and click on Ok.

So now the test object will identify all the edit boxes that starts with q followed by any characters.

3. How to read XML file in UFT?

```
Set objXMLDoc =
CreateObject("Microsoft.XMLDOM")
objXMLDoc.async = False
```

```
objXMLDoc.load("books.xml")
Set parentel= objXMLDoc.documentElement
Set cList =
parentel.getElementsByTagName("book")
For Each E In cList
        print E.Text
Next
```

This example will print all xml node values in UFT.

How to take a screenshot in UFT?

In UFT, when we execute the test cases, test cases may fail due to valid / invalid defects. They may also fail due to script issues or any other issues like network failure.

After the test execution ends, We only have the html reports or UFT results with us which does not give clear picture about the status of application. To solve this problem we can take the snapshot of the application when any test step fails.

Example - Below code will take the screen shot. You can insert this code anywhere you want to take the screen shot.

```
Window("xyz").CaptureBitmap
"c:\screenshots\abc.png",True
```

In above code we are storing the png image file to c drive location. Second parameter tells whether to overwrite existing file.

Thus you can use capturebitmap method of any object to take the screen shot.

Dictionary Object in UFT with Example

Dictionary object is used to store the data in key-item pairs in UFT.

A Dictionary object is just like an associative array.
It stores the data in the form of key-item pairs.
Each key has some data item associated with it.
Key can be integer or string format.
Data item can be integer or string or array of variants. It may contain other dictionary itself.

Methods of Dictionary Object

1. Add -------> Adds new key-item pair in the dictionary object
2. Exists ----> returns true if the given key exists in the dictionary object
3. Items -----> returns the array containing all items in the dictionary object
4. Keys ------> returns the array containing all keys in the dictionary object
5. Remove ----> removes the key-item pair with given key from the dictionary object
6. RemoveAll -> removes all key-item pairs from the dictionary object

Properties of Dictionary Object

1. Count--------> returns the total number of keys in the dictionary object
2. Item---------> assigns or returns the item value with given key from the dictionary object
3. Key----------> sets the new key value for the given key
4. CompareMode -> assigns or returns the comparison mode for comparing string keys in a Dictionary object.

Example with dictionary object in UFT

```
'create new dictionary object
Set dictionaryObject =
CreateObject("Scripting.Dictionary")

'add some key-item pairs
dictionaryObject.Add "1", "Sagar"
dictionaryObject.Add "2", "Amol"
dictionaryObject.Add "3", "Ganesh"

'Display data in the dictionary
for each k in dictionaryObject.keys

 print k & " - " &
dictionaryObject.item(k)

next

'Remove the key-item pair with key = 1
from the dictionary object
dictionaryObject.Remove("1")

'Remove all key-item pairs from the
dictionary object
dictionaryObject.RemoveAll
```

```
'Release the object
Set dictionaryObject = nothing
```

Explain RegExp Object in UFT.

RegExp is a very important object in UFT that can be used to find the patterns in given string using regular expressions.

This object can be created using below syntax.

```
Set regExpObject = New RegExp
```

RegExp Object supports below properties.

Global Property   - a pattern should match all occurrences in string or just the first one
IgnoreCase Property - specifies if the search is case-sensitive or not
Pattern Property   - Sequence of literal characters and special characters (Meta Characters like *,?,+,\b,\d,\n etc)

RegExp Object supports below methods.

Test Method   - returns true if the pattern is found in the given string
Execute Method - returns a Matches collection containing a Match object(having properties firstindex and value) for each match found in string.

Replace Method - replaces the matched values in the given string by another value

Sample Example on Execute method.

```
Set regExpObject = New RegExp
   search_string = "MS dhoni is very
lucky cricketer"
   regExpObject.Pattern = "lucky"

   regExpObject.Ignorecase = true
   regExpObject.Global = true

 Set matches   =
regExpObject.execute(search_string)

 For each match in matches
   print  match.firstIndex & " - " &
match.value
 Next
```

In above example we are trying to find the pattern "lucky" in the given string "MS dhoni is very lucky cricketer". We are also printing the position where the match is found.

How to open any website(URL) in browser (IE,chrome, firefox) in UFT?

You can use below code to open an url in UFT.

```
url = "www.google.co.in"
```

```
SystemUtil.Run "iexplore.exe" , url ,,,3
SystemUtil.Run "firefox.exe" , url ,,,3
SystemUtil.Run "chrome.exe" , url ,,,3
```

Above code will open url in all browsers.

In plain vbscript you can use below code to open a url.

```
Set o = createobject("wscript.shell")
o.Run "chrome.exe www.makaan.com"
o.Run "firefox.exe www.makaan.com"
Set o = nothing
```

www.ingramcontent.com/pod-product-compliance
Lightning Source LLC
Chambersburg PA
CBHW061026050326
40689CB00012B/2708